I0842450

"Animal Kingdom Adventures"

Exploring the Fascinating World of Animals

Volume 1

"Animal Kingdom Adventures"
Exploring the Fascinating World of Animals
Bennie Thomas II © 2023

Table of Contents

Rock-a-Bye Rhino: A Lullaby for the Mighty Horned One"

(Verse 1)

Rock-a-bye rhino, in the land of savanna,
With your mighty horn, you rock your bandana,
Big and strong, you'll slumber deep,
Dreaming of tasty leaves, oh what a treat!

(Chorus)

Rock-a-bye rhino, your skin is gray and tough,
With two sharp horns, you've got the stuff,
And when you snore, the others all know,
The rhino's fast asleep, ready for the show!

(Verse 2)

Did you know, dear rhino, you're one of a kind,
Poor eyesight, but smell and hearing, you'll find,
When you run, you never make a moo,
As fast as a car, oh my, who knew!

(Chorus)

Rock-a-bye rhino, your skin is gray and tough,
With two sharp horns, you've got the stuff,
And when you snore, the others all know,
The rhino's fast asleep, ready for the show!

"Animal Kingdom Adventures"
Exploring the Fascinating World of Animals
Bennie Thomas II © 2023

So close your eyes, and dream the night away,
The world awaits you with a new day,
Goodnight, dear rhino, sleep tight,
For tomorrow, you'll be back to rule with might!

"Animal Kingdom Adventures"
Exploring the Fascinating World of Animals
Bennie Thomas II © 2023

"Lullaby of the Lion: A Sleepy Song for the King of the Jungle"

(Verse 1)
Lullaby dear lion, in the jungle tonight
With your mighty roar, you rule with might
You may be the king of the jungle, but for now you'll
rest and dream of hunting down your next big test

(Chorus)
Lullaby of the lions, with your golden mane
You're the strongest cat, it's a lion's claim to fame
And when you purr, the other animals know
That the lion's asleep, and ready for a show

(Verse 2)
Did you know, that lions are a social type?
They live in prides, and never say "goodbye"
And when they hunt, they work together like a
machine
With cooperation, they can chase down the biggest
scene

(Chorus)
Lullaby of the lions, with your golden mane
You're the strongest cat, it's a lion's claim to fame
And when you purr, the other animals know
That the lion's asleep, and ready for a show

"Animal Kingdom Adventures"
Exploring the Fascinating World of Animals
Bennie Thomas II © 2023

So close your eyes, and let the dreams come true
And know that when you wake, the jungle is waiting
for you
Goodnight lion, sweet dreams and sleep tight
And know that tomorrow, you'll be back to rule with
might!

"Animal Kingdom Adventures"
Exploring the Fascinating World of Animals
Bennie Thomas II © 2023

"Dreaming with the Dolphins: A Lullaby for Our Underwater Friends"

(Verse 1)
Dreaming with the dolphins, in the ocean blue
With their playful songs, they sing to you
Graceful and free, they swim so fast
And bring joy to all, that's meant to last

(Chorus)
Dreaming with the dolphins, in the deep blue sea
With their laughter and play, they swim so carefree
And when they sing, the waves sing back
Bringing peace and joy, to the ocean's track

(Verse 2)
Did you know, that dolphins are smart creatures?
They use echolocation, to communicate with their features
And when they play, they have fun with style
Jumping and twirling, they cover many a mile!

(Chorus)
Dreaming with the dolphins, in the deep blue sea
With their laughter and play, they swim so carefree
And when they sing, the waves sing back
Bringing peace and joy, to the ocean's track

So close your eyes, and let the dreams come true
And know that when you wake, the ocean is waiting
for you
Goodnight dolphins, sweet dreams and sleep tight
And know that tomorrow, you'll be back to play in the
light!

"Animal Kingdom Adventures"
Exploring the Fascinating World of Animals
Bennie Thomas II © 2023

"Hush Little Panda: A Lullaby for the Black and White Bear"

(Verse 1)
Hush little panda, don't you cry
Snuggled up in your bamboo, as the night goes by
With your black and white fur, you're a bear so rare
And when you eat bamboo, you show that you care!

(Chorus)
Hush little panda, go to sleep
And dream of munching on bamboo, as your
bedtime treat
And when you wake, you'll be as bright
As the black and white fur, that shines so bright

(Verse 2)
Did you know, that pandas are picky eaters?
Bamboo is their main dish, and leaves them quite the
achievers
But when they play, they do it with flair
Rolling and tumbling, without a single care

(Chorus)
Hush little panda, go to sleep
And dream of munching on bamboo, as your
bedtime treat
And when you wake, you'll be as bright
As the black and white fur, that shines so bright

(Outro)
So close your eyes, and let the dreams come true
And know that when you wake, the bamboo is waiting
for you
Goodnight panda, sweet dreams and sleep tight
And know that tomorrow, you'll be back to play and
take a bite!

"Giraffe Lullaby: A Tall Tale for the Gentle Giants of the Savannah"

Verse 1:

Lullaby and goodnight, to the gentle giants of the
savannah,
With necks long and legs tall, they're a sight to see.
In the African grasslands, they roam and roam,
Munching leaves from the tallest trees, as they're at
home.

Chorus:

Giraffe, giraffe, with a neck so high,
You can reach the tallest leaves, soaring to the sky.
With spots so unique, you stand out from the crowd,
Giraffe, giraffe, sleep tight, sleep tight, you gentle
giant of the
Savannah night.

Verse 2:

Did you know, giraffes have blue tongues?
Long and slim, they help them pick leaves with ease.
And with hearts that weigh over 20 pounds,
They pump blood up to their heads, with a great big
sound.

Chorus:

Giraffe, giraffe, with a neck so high,
You can reach the tallest leaves, soaring to the sky.
With spots so unique, you stand out from the crowd,
Giraffe, giraffe, sleep tight, sleep tight, you gentle
giant of the Savannah night.

"Animal Kingdom Adventures"
Exploring the Fascinating World of Animals
Bennie Thomas II © 2023

So close your eyes, little one, and rest your head,
Dream of giraffes, tall and proud, around your bed.
And when you wake, with a stretch and a yawn,
Remember the gentle giants of the savannah, at
dawn.

"Animal Kingdom Adventures"
Exploring the Fascinating World of Animals
Bennie Thomas II © 2023

"Swan Song: A Lullaby for the Graceful Waterbirds"

Verse 1:
Lullaby and goodnight, to the graceful waterbirds,
With feathers white, and a long neck, they glide like words.
In the lakes and rivers, they float with ease,
Graceful and serene, just like a gentle breeze.

Chorus:
Swan, swan, with a neck so long,
You glide through the water, like a beautiful song.
With feathers so white, you light up the night,
Swan, swan, sleep tight, sleep tight, you graceful
waterbird so elegant and so bright.

Verse 2:
Did you know, swans can stay underwater for
minutes, with webbed feet, they're strong swimmers,
no need for spirits. And when they meet their mate,
they stay together for life, It's love at first sight, no
need for a second sight.

Chorus:
Swan, swan, with a neck so long,
You glide through the water, like a beautiful song.
With feathers so white, you light up the night,
Swan, swan, sleep tight, sleep tight, you graceful
waterbird so elegant and so bright.

So close your eyes, little one, and drift to sleep,
Dream of swans, gliding through the water, so deep.
And when you wake, with a smile and a stretch,
Remember the graceful waterbirds, that you can never forget.

"Elephant Dreams: A Lullaby for the Majestic Pachyderms"

Verse 1:

Lullaby and goodnight, to the majestic pachyderms,
With trunks long and ears wide, they make us squirm.
In the African savannah, they roam and play,
Majestic and strong, they light up the day.

Chorus:

Elephant, elephant, with a trunk so grand,
You trumpet your way, across the land.
With memories so strong, you never forget,
Elephant, elephant, sleep tight, sleep tight, your trunk is so strong we will never have spite.

Verse 2:

Did you know, elephants are the largest land animals,
With skin so thick, they're tough as nails and handle.
And their trunks are like Swiss army knives,
With the ability to pick, and spray, and squirt, and fight.

Chorus:

Elephant, elephant, with a trunk so grand,
You trumpet your way, across the land.
With memories so strong, you never forget,
Elephant, elephant, sleep tight, sleep tight, your trunk is so strong we will never have spite.

So close your eyes, little one, and rest your head,
Dream of elephants, stomping their feet, and
trumpeting instead.
And when you wake, with a stretch and a yawn,
Remember the majestic pachyderms, at dawn.

"Kangaroo Kapi: A Lullaby for Our Aussie Jumpers"

Verse 1:

Lullaby and goodnight, to our Aussie jumpers,
With legs so strong, they'll make you thumpers.
In the outback, they hop and play,
With babies in their pouch, they're never far away.

Chorus:

In the meadow you play, from dusk until dawn,
Your legs are so springy, your hops go on and on.
Your fur is so soft, your tail sways like a vine,
Kangaroo, kangaroo, rest now, it's bedtime.

Verse 2:

Did you know, kangaroos can jump over 30 feet,
With tails to balance, they can't be beat.
And they can go for days, without taking a drink,
Storing water in their bodies, it's a survival trick.

Chorus:

In the meadow you play, from dusk until dawn,
Your legs are so springy, your hops go on and on.
Your fur is so soft, your tail sways like a vine,
Kangaroo, kangaroo, rest now, it's bedtime.

Outro:

**So close your eyes, little one, and rest your head,
Dream of kangaroos, jumping in the outback, ahead.
And when you wake, with a stretch and a yawn,
Remember our Aussie jumpers, at dawn.**

"Animal Kingdom Adventures"
Exploring the Fascinating World of Animals
Bennie Thomas II © 2023

Bearly Sleeping: "A Lullaby for the Soft and Cuddly Bears"

Verse 1:

Lullaby and goodnight, to the soft and cuddly bears,
With fur so fluffy, they'll chase away your fears.
In the forests and caves, they roam and play,
Snuggling and sleeping, all through the day.

Chorus:

Bear, bear, with a growl so deep,
You hug and you snuggle, and fall fast asleep.
With fur so warm, you're a cuddly delight,
Bear, bear, sleep tight, sleep tight, wishing you
nothing but a good night.

Verse 2:

Did you know, bears have a fantastic sense of smell,
And can smell food from miles away, it's quite well.
And when they hibernate, they don't need to eat,
They live off their fat, so cozy and sweet.

Chorus:

Bear, bear, with a growl so deep,
You hug and you snuggle and fall fast asleep.
With fur so warm, you're a cuddly delight,
Bear, bear, sleep tight, sleep tight, wishing you
nothing but a good night.

**So close your eyes, little one, and dream of bears,
Snuggling and sleeping, without a care.
And when you wake, with a stretch and a smile,
Remember the soft and cuddly bears, you'll never
forget them, all the while.**

"Animal Kingdom Adventures"
Exploring the Fascinating World of Animals
Bennie Thomas II © 2023

"Lullaby of the Jungle: A Sleepy Song for the Wild and Wonderful Animals of the Rainforest"

Verse 1:
Lullaby and goodnight, to the wild and wonderful,
In the rainforest, they play and they ponder.
With monkeys a-swinging, and snakes so sneak.
They'll take you on an adventure, oh so sweet.

Chorus:
The moon and stars light up the way,
As night turns into day.
The jungle awakes with a rustle and a stir,
Jungle, jungle, sleep tight, you're secure.

Verse 2:
Did you know, the rainforest is home to many species,
From jaguars to parrots, and monkeys, to bees.
And the leaves are so big, they block out the sun,
Making it always cool, like a shady retreat, isn't it
fun?

Chorus:
The moon and stars light up the way,
As night turns into day.
The jungle awakes with a rustle and a stir,
Jungle, jungle, sleep tight, you're secure.

"Animal Kingdom Adventures"
Exploring the Fascinating World of Animals
Bennie Thomas II © 2023

Dear Little Tondra, Tunisha, Mikayla, Ariana and Malaysia,

I wanted to take a moment to express my heartfelt gratitude to each of you for inspiring me to write "Animal Kingdom Adventures: Discovering the Wonders of the Animal World." Your boundless curiosity and enthusiasm for animals helped me create a captivating children's book that takes young readers on a magical journey through the animal kingdom. Keep inspiring me with all you accomplish through life. Your uncle loves you very much.

Bennie Thomas II

www.ingramcontent.com/pod-product-compliance
Lightning Source LLC
Chambersburg PA
CBHW040102240726
48664CB00022B/1246